SCHOOL

YARNS

AND

HoWLERS

SCHOOL YARNS AND HOWLERS

Summersdale Publishers Ltd
46 West Street
Chichester
West Sussex
PO19 1RP
UK

www.summersdale.com

Printed and bound by CPI Group (UK) Ltd, Croydon, CR0 4YY

ISBN: 978-1-84953-318-8

Substantial discounts on bulk quantities of Summersdale books are available to corporations, professional associations and other organisations. For details contact Summersdale Publishers by telephone: +44 (0) 1243 771107, fax: +44 (0) 1243 786300 or email: nicky@summersdale.com.

SCHOOL

YARNS

HOWLERS

Dickie Archer

CONTENTS

INTRODUCTION

School days are the happiest of our lives – at least that's what our mothers told us. Then they bundled us off to spend a significant portion of our childhood trapped in dusty rooms with stern-looking grown-ups who demanded we stop enjoying ourselves to focus on studying some fellow called 'the Bard' or peculiar things called 'quadratic equations'.

If children think they have it bad today, they would do well to remember the time when school was really tough – maths *without* a calculator, essays *without* the aid of a word processor with automatic spelling correction; not to mention some dreaded thing called the cane. School in the 'olden days' was certainly challenging, but it was also a source of great merriment for teachers and pupils alike – there was enough schoolyard silliness and classroom calamity to bring a smile to the face of even the most serious student or po-faced pedagogue.

7

With this in mind, it's time to pack your satchel, straighten your tie and prepare yourself for a bit of old-fashioned high jinks with this collection of classic school yarns and howlers – just don't get caught reading it while you're meant to be learning your times tables!

SPELLING SLIP-UPS

Pants grow well in dark, damp conditions.

I like playing cricket and practise lots so I am god at it.

The Isle of Wight is off the south coast of England. A fairy can take you there.

Peasant shooting is a common pastime in the countryside.

We wouldn't have the police, schools or many other things if we didn't pay our taxis.

———

The French Revolution was started by the people revolving because they didn't like the monarchy.

———

A ship's window is known as a pothole.

During witch trials in the Middle Ages, people suspected of being in league with the devil were burned at the steak.

People in Ireland speak both English and Garlic.

Science experiments should always be performed in a special lavatory.

Before the invention of the firearm, a common weapon of war was the hoe and arrow.

If one doesn't clean one's teeth regularly, it will result in plague.

The equator can be conceived of as an imaginary lion running around the world.

On a long walk, it is pleasant to take a break and rest in the shade of a corpse.

Blood flows through the alimentary canal and then into the abdominal calamity.

The Boar War was fought between South African Boars and the British Empire.

Florence Nightingale was known as the 'Lady with the Lump'.

Evidence of Romans in Britain can be found everywhere. Good examples are Roman farts.

To be an accountant, one has to be very good at moths.

Plato and Socrates were both philosophers, and they both originated from Grease.

Gravity is a farce that draws
objects towards each other.

—

Before the invention of refrigerators,
food was kept cool in panties.

—

Sir Walter Raleigh, a favourite of Queen
Elizabeth, was a famous exploder.

**The suffragettes took
action in order
to win the vole.**

Two halves make a whale.

When someone has had an accident you should bondage them.

Blowing is a popular sport from America.

St Paul's Cathedral is a big church in London with a doomed roof.

Electric pythons are very dangerous
and can kill you if you get too close.

Moses came down from Mount Cyanide
with the Ten Commandments.

Gases, when they come into contact with
a cold surface, create compensation.

Due to the immense size of the universe, it is very likely that there are alans somewhere on another planet.

Without their wigs, birds would be unable to fly.

In olden days it was believed that the earth was flat, but now we know it is as fear.

Many homes are warmed by an open coat fire in the living room.

A committee is a decision-making body that is led by a choir.

Aunteaters are South American mammals
that use their long tongue to eat aunts.

Pineapples grow on pine trees.

The earth makes a resolution
on its axis every 24 hours.

A key part of working
in a shop is the art
of widow dressing.

The first book in the Bible is called Guinesses.

In a Feudal system, nobles have more money than pheasants.

———

Parasites are the people who live in Paris.

———

Humidity towards others is something that Christians try to preserve.

Light passes into the eye through its lens
and is then focussed on the rectum.

1066 was the start of the Mormon
Conquest of Britain.

A woman who is married to a
butler is called a buttress.

**A cow is milked
by its rudders.**

A baby turkey is called a goblet.

Some people in France wear berries on their heads.

Everyone was amazed when Jesus was erased from the dead.

Anthropology is the study of ants.

Queen Victoria sat on the thorn
for the longest time in history.

A doctor who saves animals
is called a vegetarian.

In Australia they have wild
dogs called drongos.

**Jacob, the son of
Isaac, was guilty of
stealing his brother's
birthmark.**

CLASSROOM
CLANGERS

TEACHER: What was the first thing
James I did when he came to the throne?
PUPIL: He sat on it, Sir.

———

TEACHER: Harris, what is an equinox?
HARRIS: Please, Miss, half a
horse and half a bull!

———

TEACHER: Use the word
'census' in a sentence.
PUPIL: Please, Sir: It was dark and we
moved quietly so they couldn't census.

TEACHER: Today we will be studying *A Portrait of the Artist as a Young Man* by James Joyce.

PUPIL: But Sir, this is an English lesson, not art.

TEACHER: For which work is Robert
Louis Stevenson best known?
PUPIL: Please Sir, Stephenson's Rocket.

———

TEACHER: Use the word
'denial' in a sentence.
PUPIL: Denial is the longest
river in the world.

———

TEACHER: What is the difference
between lightning and electricity?
PUPIL: We don't have to pay for lightning.

TEACHER: How are your
English lessons going?
PUPIL: Brilliant, Sir; Teacher says
he can't teach me anything!

———

TEACHER: What did the Israelites
do on coming out of the Red Sea.
PUPIL: Dried themselves, Sir.

———

TEACHER: Where is it that
Popes are crowned?
PUPIL: On their heads, Sir.

After a pupil returns from time off due to illness:

TEACHER: You're quite far behind on your history work. How long is it you've been absent for?

PUPIL: Since the Renaissance, Miss.

TEACHER: What is meant by 'Glass going up'?

PUPIL: Somebody drinking a nice glass of beer, Sir.

TEACHER: Stone Age, Bronze
Age – what comes next?
PUPIL: Old Age, Sir?

TEACHER: What do you think the
Duke of Wellington would be doing
today if he were still alive?
PUPIL: Drawing his pension, Miss.

TEACHER: Grey, can you name the seasons?
GREY: Football, cricket, hunting and festive.

TEACHER: Which waterway connects
the Mediterranean to the Red Sea?
PUPIL: The Sewage Canal, Sir.

TEACHER: What is a pygmy?
PUPIL: Please, Miss, is it a cross
between you and pig?

TEACHER: How large was
King Solomon's harem?
PUPIL: He had 300 porcupines, Sir.

TEACHER: Why is it that giraffes have such long necks?

PUPIL: Please, Miss, because their heads are so far away from their bodies.

TEACHER: How would you describe Shakespeare's *A Midsummer Night's Dream*?

PUPIL: It's a comedy and error, Sir.

TEACHER: What contains the
Scorpion, the Ram, the Bull, the Lion
and the Crab and begins with Z?
PUPIL: Please, Sir, the zoo.

TEACHER: Who joined Noah on the ark?
PUPIL: Joan of Arc, Miss.

TEACHER: What is the
function of the pancreas?
PUPIL: Sir, it's a big railway
station in London.

TEACHER: What is it that moths eat?
PUPIL: They eat holes in clothes, Sir.

———

TEACHER: Higgins, where would
you expect to find an oboe?
HIGGINS: Oboes live on the streets, Sir.

———

TEACHER: What are the defining
characteristics of a polygon?
PUPIL: Please, Miss, it's a
parrot, but it's dead.

TEACHER: Anybody wishing to take part in voluntary elocution lessons must see me after class.

PUPIL: But, Miss, doesn't elocution make your hair stand on end and kill you?

TEACHER: Who was the first woman on earth?

PUPIL: Please, Sir, I don't know.

TEACHER: Think of the apple story...

PUPIL: Ah yes, I have it — Granny Smith!

TEACHER: If you had half a crown
and you asked your father for another,
how much would you have?
PUPIL: Half a crown, Sir.
TEACHER: Are you sure?
PUPIL: Yes, Sir. I'm sure my father
couldn't afford to give me half a crown.

TEACHER: It's clear to me that you haven't
studied your geography. What's your excuse?
PUPIL: Well, Sir, my mother says the
world is changing every day – so I
decided to wait until it settles down.

TEACHER: You aren't paying attention to
me, Forsyth. Are you having trouble hearing?
FORSYTH: No, Sir, I'm having
trouble listening!

TEACHER: Williams, were you
copying Davies' sums?
WILLIAMS: No, Sir, just
seeing if he got his right!

———

TEACHER: Does anyone know
which month has 28 days?
PUPIL Please, Sir, all of them!

———

TEACHER: Benson, please don't
whistle while studying.
BENSON: Pardon me, Sir, but I'm
not studying – only whistling.

TEACHER:
When was Rome built?

PUPIL: At night, Miss.

TEACHER: Why did you
say that, my dear?

PUPIL: Because my grandfather
always says that Rome wasn't
built in a day.

TEACHER: What is the most common phrase used in school?

PUPIL: I don't know...

TEACHER: That is correct!

TEACHER: Now, can anyone tell me how many seconds there are in a year?
PUPIL: Twelve, Miss: 2nd of January, 2nd of February and one in all of the other months.

———

TEACHER: Hopkins, this is the fifth time I've had to tell you off this week – what have you got to say about that?
HOPKINS: Thank heavens it's Friday, Sir!

———

TEACHER: Can anyone give me the name of a liquid that will not freeze?
PUPIL: Please, Sir: hot water.

TEACHER: Who can tell me the plural of 'mouse'?

PUPIL: I can, Miss, it's 'mice'.

TEACHER: Very good. Now, what is the plural of 'baby'?

PUPIL: Twins, Miss!

SCHOOL YARNS

A Helping Hand

Two pupils, Barlow and Hendrick, were just putting the finishing touches on an assignment they'd been working on for weeks, when Barlow spilt a large pot of red ink all over the pages.

'Darn it,' Barlow exclaimed, 'I could kick myself!'

To which Hendrick swiftly replied, 'Here, old chap, let me do it for you!'

An Amazing Mind

In Biology class, the teacher was becoming increasingly frustrated with a pupil who kept coming up with the most ludicrous answers to questions on the study of the human brain. After a typically inane response, the teacher was at his wit's end: 'Jenkins, my boy, your mind is truly amazing.'

'Why do you say that, Sir?' the boy replied.

'Amazing because it maintains constant activity from the moment you wake up, and never stops working until you are required to answer a question in class!'

Good Heavens

A teacher was attempting to explain the idea of Heaven to her class of infants.

'Now,' said the teacher, 'who would want to go to Heaven?' All the hands in the class went up apart from one. 'Arthur,' the teacher asked, 'don't you want to go to Heaven?'

'I do, Miss,' Arthur replied, 'only my mother told me to always go straight home after school.'

Right Angles

'Now, class,' the arithmetic teacher said sternly, 'having explained the basic principles of thorough and careful procedure in your calculations, I will ask again: what is the single most important thing a pupil needs to get top marks in geometry?'

'Please, Sir,' one girl replied, 'the right angles, Sir.'

The Merchant of Mischief

A visiting professor was giving a special lesson on Shakespeare's *The Merchant of Venice*. The professor, who happened to be quite rotund, divulged that he had once featured in a performance of this particular play, and asked, 'What part do you think I took, class?'

One mischievous pupil replied, half hiding, 'Please, Sir, was it the pound of flesh?'

Island Daze

In a geography lesson the teacher asked, 'Who can give me the definition of an island?'

One pupil replied, 'Please, Miss, it's a mass of land surrounded by water on all but one side.'

'All but one side?' the teacher asked, surprised.

'Yes, Miss – all but the top side, Miss.'

The Correct Egg-spression

An English teacher was attempting to explain gender in nouns. 'Now, Winthorpe,' the teacher asked, 'in terms of grammar, how might one describe the word "egg"?'

'A noun, Sir,' Winthorpe replied.

'Very good,' said the teacher. 'And what is its gender? Masculine, feminine or neuter?'

Winthorpe hesitated: 'Well, Sir,' he replied, 'it's not really possible to tell... until it's hatched.'

Differences

A lesson on different cultures came to a discussion about Quakers. 'Who can tell me something that is peculiar to the Quakers?' the teacher asked.

'Their speech, Sir' one boy replied.

'Correct! And what is it about their speech that is different?' the teacher prompted.

'Please, Sir... the Quakers don't swear like we do!' the boy said.

A Sticky Predicament

A young boy in junior class was sitting at his desk chewing away on some gum. His teacher noticed this and demanded he take himself over to the waste paper bin and throw the gum away. The boy reluctantly got up, made his way over the bin and placed the gum inside, wrapped in a piece of paper. He made his way back to his seat with a worried look on his face.

'What is it, boy?' the teacher asked.

'Well, Sir, I think I'm in for it when I get home; my brother only lent me the gum for the afternoon!'

Mixed

A young lady passing the school gates saw a small girl crying and asked what the matter was. The little girl replied, 'Please, Miss, I can't find my way to school.'

'But look,' the lady said, 'all the other little school girls are going in through that door there, that must be where you need to go!'

The girl still looked dismayed. 'But, Miss,' she replied, 'I'm not a little girl, I'm a mixed infant.'

A Harsh Sentence

At a school where wayward young boys are taught to be more civil and obedient, a teacher was giving a lesson on the solar system. He explained how, as a result of its distance from the sun, Mars takes 687 Earth days to make one full orbit of the sun. Hence, a year on Mars is 687 days long.

'Please, Sir,' one bright spark interrupted, 'I wouldn't like to live there.'

'And why ever not, boy?' the teacher enquired.

'Well, Sir,' the boy said, 'imagine being stuck in a place like this for *four* years!'

Uniform Confusion

A boy arrived at school in his raincoat with a very worried look on his face. Just before the bell rang he was seen to dash into the bathroom. Arriving a few minutes late for the class, the boy walked in to see the teacher and the rest of the children aghast.

'Child,' the teacher said, 'where on earth are your trousers?'

Timidly the boy answered, 'Well, Miss, when I asked the school receptionist what uniform I had to wear, she said I must wear a clean shirt and tie – but she didn't say anything about trousers!'

Mouth Organ

Upon returning for a new term the class was asked to take it in turn to describe the presents they had received for Christmas. 'Victoria,' the teacher said, please tell the class about one of your Christmas presents.'

'Well, I was very lucky indeed. I got a mouth organ and it's the most rewarding present I've ever received!'

'And why is it the most rewarding present you've ever received, Victoria?' the teacher asked.

'Well, Miss, every time I play it, Mother gives me half a crown to stop!'

What's in a Name?

During a history lesson a teacher pointed out that surnames are often derived from the trade of one's ancestors – for example, a Smith may have relatives who worked with iron, a Saddler may have ancestors who worked making seats for horses, etc. Turning to one boy, the teacher asked, 'What do you think your ancestors were, Webb?'

'Please, Sir,' the boy answered, 'I suppose they were some sort of spider?'

Nothing to Sniff At

A young girl was at the front of the class was sniffing repeatedly, so much so that it was distracting the teacher from her work. Being able to stand the noise no longer, the teacher abruptly asked the child, 'Have you a handkerchief, my dear?' To which the girl replied, 'Yes, Miss, but Mother said I shouldn't share it with anybody.'

Keep Swinging

In gym class, two boys were having a boxing match. One boy was swinging punches like fury but was not landing any. At the end of the round he asked the games master how he was doing. 'Not very well, I'm afraid, young man,' said the games master. 'But keep it up, you might give your opponent a cold from all the air you're pushing his way!'

A Game of Two Halves

'I say,' one senior asked a fellow pupil, 'are you going to watch the school rugby match this afternoon?'

'No,' his chum said, 'it's a jolly great waste of time. I can even tell you the score before the game starts.'

'Heavens, can you really? What is it then?'

'Before the game starts: nil–nil.'

A Notable Absence

A child returned home looking glum after receiving his exam results at school. His father asked him what the matter was: 'Well, Father, I'm afraid I didn't do very well on the science exam,' the boy said.

'And why was that, son?' the father asked.

'Absence, Father,' the boy replied.

'What?! You were absent from the exam?'

'No, Father, but the boy who usually sits next to me was.'

Board Stiff

The geography teacher noticed that one of his pupils was not paying attention to the diagram he had drawn on the blackboard. To get the child's attention the teacher rapped the desk with a ruler and shouted, 'Board, Jones – board!'

To which the boy replied, 'Y-yes, Sir… I'm afraid so!'

Labour in Vain

As punishment for speaking out of turn in class, Hopkins was ordered to clean the blackboard in the English teacher's classroom at lunchtime. The teacher, upon returning to the classroom, was amazed to see the boy still at it.

'Good heavens, Hopkins,' the teacher said, 'haven't you finished cleaning that board yet?'

'No, Sir,' Hopkins replied, 'I'm afraid the more I clean the blacker it gets!'

Adding Insult to Injury

Smith had been late for school every morning for a couple of weeks. His form master was angry with him and gave him the cane. 'Now, Smith,' he said, 'tell me why I punished you.'

'That's hardly fair, Sir,' Smith said, crying, 'first you scold me, then you give me the cane, and now you don't know what you did it for!'

Holy Garments

A mother was helping her son get ready for the first day of school. 'Now, son,' she said, 'these new clothes are expensive. I don't want you coming home after the first week with a hole in the knee of your trousers.'

'Very well, Mother,' the boy replied, 'where would you like the hole to be?'

Learning the Lingo

A teacher was giving a class about South America. After discussing the cultural diversity of the region, the teacher asked the class which language they thought was spoken in Cuba. One girl piped up: 'Please, Miss, is it "Cubic"?'

Present Tense

On the first day of school the new intake of juniors arrived for class on time, except for one boy who came wandering in 15 minutes late. The teacher found that there was nowhere for the boy to sit, so she took him to her desk and said, 'Right, Billy, just sit there for the present.' A few minutes later the teacher returned with a chair for Billy and asked him to sit himself at his desk. Billy was reluctant. 'But, Miss,' he said, 'if I move from my seat, will I still get the present?'

Lost for Words

A class had been given the task of writing a paper on the funniest thing they ever saw. The teacher noticed one boy sitting at the back, not working and demanded to know why he wasn't setting to the task. The boy answered, with a glint in his eye: 'But, Sir, the funniest thing I ever saw is just too funny for words!'

Elementary

'Now, class,' the science teacher said to his junior pupils, 'who can tell me the formula for water?' An eager pupil raised his hand in excitement and was asked to come forward to the blackboard to write it out. Hurriedly the boy came to the front of the class and wrote 'H I J K L M N O', setting the chalk down and looking very pleased with himself.

'What's this?' the teacher asked.

'Please, Sir, it's the formula for water: H to O.'

Cheesed Off

In the school canteen a boy was complaining that he didn't care for cheese with holes in. 'Don't worry,' the lunch mistress said, 'just eat the cheese and you may leave the holes on the side of your plate.'

Spitting Feathers

Two school friends were enjoying a dessert of steamed pudding and custard, when all of a sudden one turned to the other. 'I say, I believe I've found a feather in my custard!'

'Well, that makes perfect sense,' said the other friend.

'How so?'

'Well, it is Bird's custard!'

EXCUSES,
EXCUSES

Dear Sir,

Please excuse Tommy for being absent last week.
I had a baby.

Yours truly, Mrs —
P.S. It wasn't Tommy's fault.

Dear Sir,
Little Johnny came home in tears yesterday,
saying you said he was illiterate. This is
not at all true. His father and I had been
married for over a year when he was born.

Yours sincerely,
Mrs —

Dear Sir,

I offer my sincerest apologies for the way Elizabeth spoke to you yesterday. When I explained to her that you said she was a disturbing element, not a disturbing elephant, she was not nearly as angry and upset.

Yours,

Mrs —

Dear Sir,

Following my child's poor score on the history exam I must protest the exam was unfair: all the questions were about things that happened before he was born!

Yours truly,

Mr—

Dear Sir,

Many apologies that my child was not in attendance at school yesterday, he was 'very ill'.

Yours,

Mrs —

P.S. No, I didn't believe him either.

Dear Sir,
Please excuse Jimmy from being absent from
school — he has information of the lungs.
Regards,

Mr —

Dear Sir,
Please execute my son for not being in
school yesterday, he was rather unwell.
Yours truly,
Mrs —

Dear Sir,

Excuse my daughter for being late this morning. Please believe whatever story she tells you.

Yours,

Mrs —

Dear Sir,
My sincerest apologies for my son not being in
school yesterday his mother was giving birth.
I can assure you this will not happen again.
Mr —

Dear Sir,
Please excuse Anne for being absent from
school yesterday — she had an ulster in
her throat and she was in a great deal
of pain.

Dear Sir,

Please excuse Oliver for being absent yesterday; he badly bumped his head the night before. We took him to the hospital to have his head examined, and, luckily, they didn't find anything.

Mr—

Overheard in class:

Sorry I was absent yesterday, Sir, I
had to look after Mother as she was
bedridden with ten disciples.

TEACHER: Why were you absent yesterday?
PUPIL: I swallowed some wool, Sir.
TEACHER: Do you think
I'll believe that yarn?

PUPIL: Sir, would you be angry with
me for something I didn't do?
TEACHER: Of course I wouldn't.
PUPIL: Do you promise?
TEACHER: Yes.
PUPIL: I didn't do my homework.

Sorry I'm late, Sir – there are eight children in my family, but my mother set the alarm for seven.

―――

I'm afraid I can't do P.E. today, Sir. I fell out of a tree yesterday and misplaced my hip!

―――

Sorry I didn't bring my homework in yesterday, Miss, I had to go the dentist with my rotten tooth. I've brought it in today!

A pupil was performing badly in English lessons and was given a grammatically complex sentence to write out 40 times.
TEACHER: You've only copied this out 36 times. How do you expect to improve your English?
PUPIL: Please, Sir, I'm not too good at maths, neither.

I did complete my homework assignment, Miss – but my pet rabbit had babies and they were desperate for nesting material, so I had to give it up, for their sake.

TEACHER: Why are you late?
PUPIL: Actually, Sir, I'm here for tomorrow's lessons, so I'm really very early.

Sorry I was not in attendance at school yesterday; I was involved in a matter of great importance for Her Majesty's Secret Service.

Sorry I don't have my homework, Miss, I let someone copy it and they didn't give it back!

HOMEWORK HOWLERS

The population of London is very dense.

John Wycliffe translated the Bible into Middle English, because he thought that people in the Midlands weren't religious enough.

Jesus was joined by 12 opossums which followed him wherever he went.

A type of entertainment enjoyed by the Romans was watching gladiolas fight in the arena.

Gorilla warfare is a special type of conflict which most people consider to be cruel.

In Russia, the people used to be ruled by Sardines.

Dangerous animals found in Africa include lions, cheaters and lepers.

After escaping Egypt, the Israelites built and worshipped a golden calf, because they did not bring enough gold to make a golden cow.

William Gilbert was one of the first people to study eccentricity.

Knowing he had to reach the next village before nightfall, the detective set out on his well-boiled bicycle.

Herod was the King when Jesus was born, and he later had a shop in London named after him.

Chaplets are small places of worship.

The American city of Cleveland can be
found at the bottom of Lake Erie.

The Pope lives in a city-state within
the city of Rome called the vacuum.

A conjunction is a place where
two rail lines meet.

**Ships communicate
with each other by
metaphor, using flags.**

Habeas corpus was a Latin phrase used at the time of the Great Plague. It means: 'bring out your dead'.

In Roman Catholic churches, insects are burned in a censer.

Buddha founded his religion in Budapest.

In this Jane Austen novel, the main character is in search of an edible suitor.

A heavy blow to the head can cause
someone to lose their conscience.

The plural of 'forget-me-not' is 'forget-us-not'.

The patron saint of Ireland is St Patrick and
the patron saint of Britain is Union Jack.

**Venezuela is a
monster that lives
on Venus and is
always screaming.**

The zebra is an African animal that is primarily used to illustrate the letter Z.

In the Great War, a great number of people were killed, many of them mortally.

An equatorial triangle is one where all the sides and angles are the same size.

The difference between soft and hard water is that one is still water, while the other is ice.

Julius Caesar was warned by a soothsayer
to 'beware the eyes that march'.

———

Monotony is when a person
only has one spouse.

———

Moscow is the capital city of Russia,
and is inhabited by Mosquitos.

**To convert
centimetres to
metres you must
take out 'centi'.**

The Pauli Exclusion Principle outlines the areas in which parrots are not allowed.

A suspended sentence is when a man is hanged for his wrongdoing.

As well as being organised and polite, a secretary should have good tie pin skills.

A baby swan is known as a singlet.

84

Horse-drawn carrot racing was a
very popular sport in Roman times,
but it was very dangerous.

———

A giraffe is a useful way of presenting data.
Types of giraffes include line, bar and picture.

———

At the Battle of Waterloo, Napoleon didn't
expect Wellington's forces to be as strong as
they were. From this we can learn that we
should not undress to mate our enemies.

**Venice is the second
closest planet to
the sun.**

Things from the Far East are called Ornamental. Things from the West are called Accidental.

In cookery class we made a salad using lettuce, tomatoes, goats, cheese and cucumbers.

Road signs are important for safety. For example, there is a sign outside our school that says 'Slow Children Crossing'.

A gentleman is a man who gives up his seat to a lady in a public convenience.

After being left on the compost heap for many weeks, you can use your cuttings to help other plants grow.

It is said that King Arthur was killed in battle by some historians.

When his horse fell the jockey broke his arm and had to be destroyed.

The future tense of the phrase 'He drinks' is 'He is drunk'.

Alfred the Great started a chronicle, which still exists today as a newspaper.

The majority of Shakespeare's plays were horrible tragedies.

Glaciers are people who fix and replace windows.

A fibula can also be described as a little white lie.

Intensive farming is when a farmer
works for months without a day off.

If something is transparent you
can see through it – like the crack
in a door or a keyhole.

A harem is a hutch for keeping hares in.

**Cereals are very
important; my
mother watches
them every day.**

BALLY
BANTER

All that fag

A lot of effort; 'donkey work' of the kind one might leave a junior – 'fag' – to deal with.

Bad egg

A dastardly fellow; one who doesn't play fair; a rotten sort. e.g. 'We'd best avoid old Nelson, he's one bad egg.'

Bosh

Nonsense; 'pish posh'.

Dab hand

An expert at a particular activity, often one which involves one's hands or some physical skill.

Drat

Expression of annoyance or anger.

Dry-bob

A young chap who opts for cricket over boating, cf. Wet-bob.

Bosh! Forget *all that fag* about practising your Latin conjugations, Hopkins, we're off down to the river; do come and join us, *old fellow*, don't be a *bad egg!*

Duffer

A somewhat haphazard, ineffectual or undesirable fellow. E.g. 'Mr Jenkins had us doing algebra for two hours in a row last week, the old duffer.'

Ex Trumps

To 'go up to books Ex Trumps' – to go to class without preparing for the lesson.

Gone case

A lost cause; unsalvageable. E.g. 'It's no good, you've squashed your model and it's a gone case!'

Good sort

A trustworthy and reliable person.

Greaser

A cad; a sly old devil.

Hang it all

Condemn the lot; 'do away' with everything; exclamation denoting one's desire to abandon one's pursuit in frustration.

Drat – who would have guessed old Rogers would surprise us with an algebra test on the first day of term! What with me coming in *Ex Trumps*, it's *a gone case. Hang it all,* I say!

Hard lines

Bad luck.

High jinks

Boisterous fun or classroom tomfoolery of the sort that would entertain but not cause any serious offence.

I'm a Dutchman

Denotes disbelief; used for emphatic assertion of such. E.g. 'If it wasn't old Plunkett I saw chasing his dog down the road just now, I'm a Dutchman.'

Jack's delight

Play Jack's delight; to create mischief and disruption. E.g. 'Some dirty rotter has been playing Jack's delight with the laces on my cricketing boots – they're all in knots!'

Jape

A jibe; a prank; 'high jinks'.

Jings

Exclamation denoting surprise; similar to 'By Jingo!'.

Hard lines on the arithmetic exam, old chum. Perhaps it's just not your thing? Forget all of that nonsense, for now – what say we sneak into the store cupboard and surprise Miss Barlow when she comes in? A little *high jinks* should be a jolly good *jape!*

Luxer

A handsome fellow.

My stars

Expression of astonishment.

Muzz

To muse idly; to daydream.

Old fellow

Regardless of one's age, one may be addressed by a schoolyard chum as 'old fellow', by way of endearment.

Poor biz

A shame; bad luck.

Ripping

Splendid; excellent. E.g. 'Gosh, what a ripping sailboat.'

My stars, Cadby, what a *ripping* good shot! I didn't realise you were such a *dab hand* at marbles. Well done, *old fellow!*

Rotten lark

A disagreeable situation; a bad joke; mischief that is mean rather than amusing.

Rotter

An undesirable sort; one who has acted unjustly towards another.

Rustication

Suspension from school.

Snakes alive!

Expression of surprise or shock. E.g. Snakes alive, Watson. That cricket ball almost took your head clean off!

Snicks

To 'go snicks'; to share.

Tally ho

A rousing cry; an alert. Originally used by huntsmen upon spotting a fox, but more commonly used as a call to action E.g. 'Tally ho and away we go!'

I say, this boating is a *rotten lark* – I can't row for toffee. I was clearly cut to be a *dry-bob*. *Poor biz* to get lumbered with this bunch!

Thumping lot

An impressive amount or degree. E.g. 'That's a thumping lot better.'

Titching

A 'tickling' with the cane. E.g. 'It's no good – Rogers has been had up for his cheating in the arithmetic test. He'll be getting a thorough titching from the Head this afternoon.'

Wet-bob

A young chap who opts for boating over cricket, cf. Dry-bob.

PLAYGROUND
POPPYCOCK

How were the Vikings able to
send covert messages?

By Norse code.

———

Why did the teacher need to hang
a lantern in the classroom?

Because the class was so dim!

———

What kind of food do arithmetic teachers eat?

Square meals.

———

How did the boy feel after being caned?

Absolutely whacked!

Who was the most famous king to use fractions?

Henry the Eighths

What is the difference between ammonia and pneumonia?

Ammonia comes in bottles, pneumonia comes in chests.

Why are school catering staff so cruel?

Because they batter fish, beat
eggs and whip cream.

———

Why did the teacher draw on the window?

Because she wanted her lesson
to be a clear as possible.

———

What kind of tool do you need for arithmetic?

A pair of multi-pliers!

———

**What did the cross-eyed teacher
say to the head teacher?**

I can't control my pupils!

**LUCY: Our English teacher
is a peach, isn't she?**

LOUISE: Do you mean she is really nice?

LUCY: No, I mean she has a heart of stone!

What is the shortest month?

May – because it only has three letters.

**What is a butterfly's favourite
subject at school?**

Mothmatics.

Why does history keep repeating itself?

Because we weren't listening the first time!

BILLY: Teacher said we will have only half a day's school this morning.

BOBBY: Really? Hooray!

BILLY: He said we will have the other half this afternoon.

**What did the ink pen
say to the pencil?**

What's your point?

What kind of birds do you find in captivity?

Jailbirds.

How can one prevent diseases caused by biting insects?

Be sure not to bite any!

What do you call a person who keeps on talking when people are no longer interested?

A teacher.

Why did the girl do her maths classwork on the floor?

Because the teacher told her to do it without using tables.

What is a math teacher's favourite dessert?

Pi.

Why was the ghost of Anne Boleyn always running after the ghost of Henry VIII?

She was trying to get ahead!

What did Noah do to pass time on the ark?

He fished, but he didn't catch much because he only had two worms.

Why is remembering your English history like a classroom?

Too many rulers!

**Which English king
invented the fireplace?**

Alfred the Grate!

LUCY: How do we know that the Egyptians invented tennis?

LOUISE: I don't know.

LUCY: Because, in the Bible, it says that Joseph served in Pharaoh's court.

What did the triangle say to the circle?

You're pointless!

Why did the cyclops have to close his school?

Because he only had one pupil.

Did you hear about the two chums
playing football with peas in a saucer?

They were playing for the cup.

Why is the school football pitch always wet?

Because the players are always dribbling.

BILLY: Why do you see swimmers
swimming on their back?

BOBBY: I don't know – why is it?

BILLY: Because it's dangerous
to swim on a full stomach!

What is a runner's
favourite subject?

Jog-graphy!

Why is Shakespeare like a harsh judge?

Both of them have difficult sentences.

———

**What is the most mathematical
part of speech?**

The 'add verb'.

———

**What are the three least friendly
letters in the alphabet?**

N-M-E.

———

Which three letters are a musical instrument?

P-N-O.

LUCY: I don't think I'll bother coming back to school.

LOUISE: Why ever not?

LUCY: Our teachers aren't up to very much – all they do is ask *us* questions!

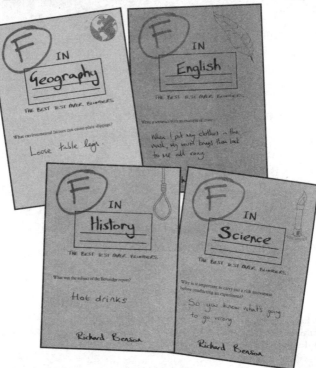

F IN SERIES

Richard Benson

The Exams are over, the results are in
and just when you thought it was safe
to go back in the classroom...

BANG! It's time for the F in... Series!

Enjoy a heady dose of hilarious answers
that canny students have given to
the trickiest exam questions.

F in Exams £6.99 (ISBN: 978 1 84024 700 8) • F in Retakes £6.99 (ISBN: 978 1 84953 313 3)
F in English £3.99 (ISBN: 978 1 84953 324 9) • F in Geography £3.99 (ISBN: 978 1 84953 325 6)
F in History £3.99 (ISBN: 978 1 84953 326 3) • F in Science £3.99 (ISBN: 978 1 84953 323 2)

THE SIXTH FORM POET

DEEP THOUGHTS AND WISE WORDS

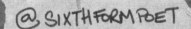

@SIXTHFORMPOET

THE SIXTH FORM POET
Deep Thoughts and Wise Words

@sixthformpoet

ISBN: 978 1 84953 319 5 Paperback £6.99

I think the Rorschach family next door look lovely, but my flatmate thinks they look like church-burning Satanists. Weird.

*I just killed a mouse.
It was a copy-cat murder.*

My friend said he'd give me £100 if I did a bungee jump. I wasn't falling for that.

Since 2011, the mysterious figure known only as Sixth Form Poet has attracted 40,000 followers on Twitter with his offbeat, witty and pun-laden observations on modern life. This collection brings together the best of his pithy one-liners and whimsical poems, brought to life with Tom McLaughlin's quirky illustrations. Dive into Sixth Form Poet's world – after all, as he says, 'It would be so cool if I had lots of fans.'

If you're interested in finding out more about our humour books, follow us on Twitter: @SummersdaleLOL

www.summersdale.com